PAINTING POPULAR BIRD CARVINGS

16 Full-Color Plates and Complete Instructions

by Anthony Hillman

DOVER PUBLICATIONS, INC., NEW YORK

Copyright © 1990 by Anthony Hillman.
All rights reserved under Pan American and International
Copyright Conventions.

Published in Canada by General Publishing Company, Ltd.,
30 Lesmill Road, Don Mills, Toronto, Ontario.
Published in the United Kingdom by Constable and Company, Ltd.,
10 Orange Street, London WC2H 7EG.

Painting Popular Bird Carvings: 16 Full-Color Plates and Complete Instructions
is a new work, first published by Dover Publications, Inc., in 1990.

Manufactured in the United States of America
Dover Publications, Inc., 31 East 2nd Street, Mineola, N.Y. 11501

Library of Congress Cataloging-in-Publication Data

Hillman, Anthony.
Painting popular bird carvings :
16 full-color plates and complete instructions / by Anthony Hillman.
p.   cm.
ISBN 0-486-26248-0
1. Birds in art. 2. Painting—Technique. I. Title.
ND1380.H55 1990
745.7′23—dc20
89-25749
CIP

Introduction and Instructions

After you have carved a songbird or similar small bird, or purchased an unfinished carving, you will want to color it faithfully according to species. My purpose in creating this book has been to provide instructions and helpful tips to anyone who wants to paint a songbird carving, no matter what his or her preferred style of painting might be. I have included sixteen full-color plates of profile and top-view illustrations as a source of accurate information on songbird coloration. As of this writing, no publication has yet provided full-color top-view reference illustrations of songbirds (except my own *Painting Songbird Carvings*, Dover 25580-8). These plates show sixteen species of songbirds in their spring plumage, when colors are at their brightest. These colors may fade to varying degrees in the fall. The birds depicted here are males. In certain species, such as the Red-breasted Nuthatch and Dark-eyed Junco (the "Slate-colored" race is shown in this book), females resemble the males in most ways but have duller coloration. In other birds, such as the Black-throated Blue Warbler, females appear very different, showing no trace of the males' livelier colors. And in yet other cases, the plumage of both sexes is very much alike. Examples in this book include the Great Crested Flycatcher, Horned Lark, Fox Sparrow and Northern Mockingbird.

Although these plates are the best painting guide available in book form and should be studied closely, the beginner cannot expect to be able to duplicate complex songbird coloration without some practice. Seldom can the exact color desired be squeezed right from a tube of paint. Many colors can be created only by the blending of pigments—and don't be afraid to experiment—but even basic colors vary depending on the type of paint (acrylics, oils, etc.) and the manufacturer.

Don't let this intimidate you. Study the instructions, plates and other sources carefully, and practice mixing and applying paints, but also do not be afraid to draw upon your own creativity. Discovering your own "recipes" is part of the fun of painting bird carvings. There is no one way to paint a carving. Gradually you will develop a personal style that you will be proud of.

RESEARCH YOUR SUBJECT

Before you begin painting, it is essential to study your subject carefully. Learn the different topographical features of a songbird (see Figure 1). This will help you remember where to apply the proper colors and markings. Feather shape and size often determine the color pattern, and therefore determine how you apply paint to your carving.

Study the color illustrations on Plates 1 through 16. These plates, which include both profiles and top views, may be removed from the book so that the appropriate one can be placed beside your carving and referred to as you paint. Supplement the plates with color photographs, and other illustrations you can find and, as much as possible, observation of live birds. This is not as difficult as it may sound. Many of the birds depicted in this book are frequent visitors to birdhouses, birdbaths and feeders. If you can observe a bird as it bathes, you will have an excellent opportunity to study at close range the groupings and structure of feathers that are common to all songbirds. In the summer, birdhouses will attract breeding birds of certain species, such as the Great Crested Flycatcher and Downy Woodpecker. Feeders are especially good for attracting wintering birds such as sparrows, juncos and nuthatches. If possible, place birdhouses and feeders near a convenient observation point—a window, for example (but out of reach of potential predators). Even if you are an apartment-house dweller in a large city, a

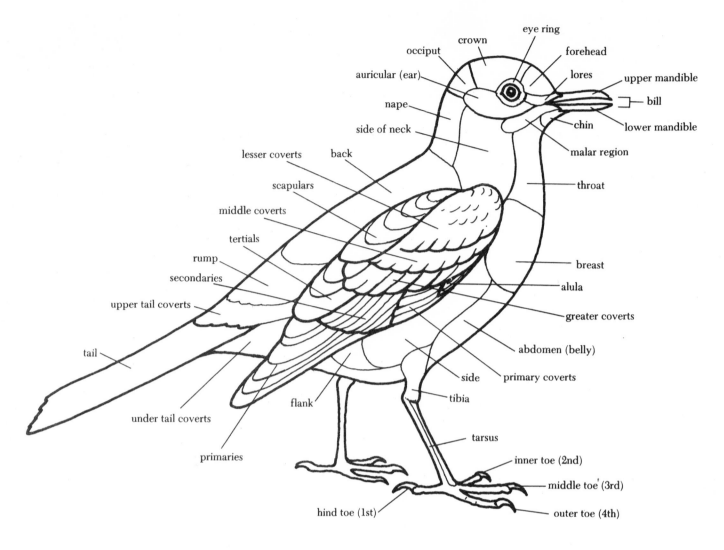

Fig. 1. Topography of a Songbird (*American Robin*)

trip to a nearby park in fall or winter will, at the very least, afford you a close look at sparrows or juncos hunting for seeds on the ground. (Note: To avoid confusion, you should be aware that the House Sparrow, so abundant in our cities, is an introduced Old World species unrelated to our native sparrows. Even in the largest cities, however, there are also some native sparrows, which generally may be found in parks. Look for them on or near the ground, around dense shrubbery. Don't be discouraged: they are there!)

Thorough research is important, but I caution against just collecting photographs and other images without firsthand observation. Certain subtle aspects of form and color cannot be properly appreciated except in the living creatures themselves. Close study of these subtleties is therefore important, but it is also fun. Songbirds are a lively group of birds that are readily seen close at hand. With practice and observation, you will gradually find it becoming easier to paint realistically.

BRUSHES AND PAINTS

When choosing any art supplies, a good rule to follow is to buy the best, or at least the best you can afford. This rule applies especially to brushes, since the brush is the instrument that gets the paint onto the surface of your carving. A wide variety of brushes is available for any paint medium you use. Figure 2 illustrates some types of brushes I find useful for painting bird carvings. If brushes of the type you desire are not available locally, write for catalogs from some of the major art-supply firms. It will be futile to attempt to paint with inferior brushes.

Through the years I have become partial to sign-painting and lettering brushes. The longer bristles on these brushes hold more paint and make it easier to control long, delicate lines. They also help keep paint from getting up into the ferrule, an important advantage when working with acrylics (for which your brush also should have a soft, white, nylon type of bristle).

(Instructions continue after plates.)

Plate 1. Mourning Dove

Plate 2. Barn Swallow

Plate 3. Northern Mockingbird

Plate 4. Downy Woodpecker

Plate 5. Horned Lark

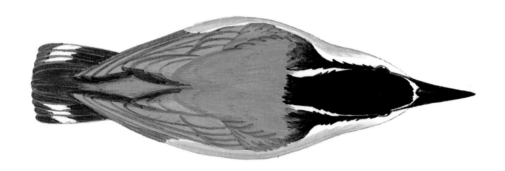

Plate 6. Red-breasted Nuthatch

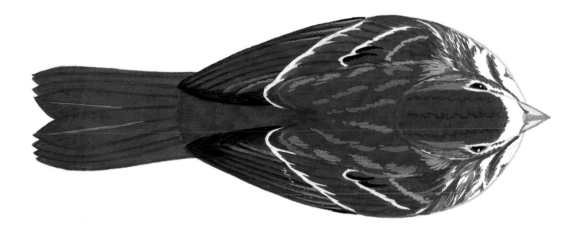

Plate 7. Fox Sparrow

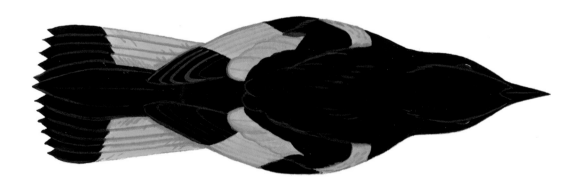

Plate 8. American Redstart

Plate 9. White-throated Sparrow

Plate 10. Rufous-sided Towhee

Plate 11. Great Crested Flycatcher

Plate 12. Eastern Meadowlark

Plate 13. Scarlet Tanager

Plate 14. Mountain Bluebird

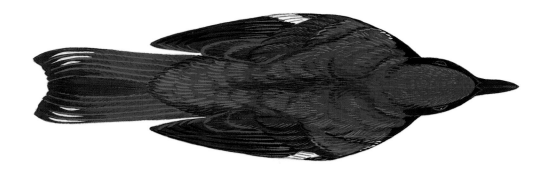

Plate 15. Black-throated Blue Warbler

Plate 16. Dark-eyed ("Slate-colored") Junco

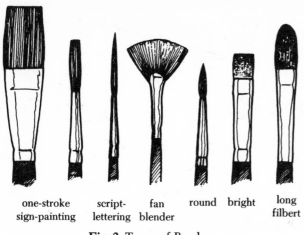

one-stroke
sign-painting   script-lettering   fan blender   round   bright   long filbert

Fig. 2. Types of Brushes

The "fan blender" is another useful brush, both for blending colors and for "dry-brush" technique. With this type of brush, I prefer white oil bristles, even for acrylic paints, as the stiffer bristles maintain the proper fan shape.

For applying large, solid areas of color, the larger-size "flats" (brushes with flattened ferrules) are the most useful. These brushes deliver a large quantity of paint while allowing good control where sharp edges are desirable.

In time you will find that some of your brushes are losing their shapes, their hairs twisting in every direction. Save these worn-out tools. Although they may no longer serve the specialized purposes you purchased them for, they can be invaluable for stippling and dry brushing.

Just as different kinds of brushes serve different purposes, different types of paint have different properties and produce different effects. Oil paints have the major disadvantage of taking a long time to dry. This can also be an advantage, however, as it permits colors to be blended to perfection. And if you make a mistake, the area can be wiped clean to start over again. If drying time is of no concern, you may prefer oils, for they produce a rich, almost sensual, gloss that seems to be obtainable with no other medium.

The two basic media for oil paint are turpentine and linseed oil. Turpentine will reduce drying time and deaden the sheen inherent in tube colors. Linseed oil, when added to paint, extends drying time and adds sheen. Several drying agents, such as cobalt drier, are available. Allowing oil paints to stand overnight on absorbent brown paper (like that used to make shopping bags) will drain off some of the linseed oil, as is preferred by some wood carvers.

Acrylic paint is probably the medium most widely used by carvers of birds. It dries quickly, and brushes can be cleaned in soap and water, making acrylics more convenient than oils for most people. *It is important to remember that for acrylic paints you must use acrylic primer.*

The speed at which acrylic paints dry can be a handicap for the beginner, but practice and familiarization with the medium soon overcome this difficulty. A gel medium, available in art-supply stores, slows drying time when added to tube acrylic paints.

Tube acrylics tend to dry with a slick surface. This is not necessarily desirable. I use flat exterior house paints as the main colors of my palette. Flat acrylics offer a distinct advantage when you are painting undercoats and thin washes of color, there being less chance of running or puddles of pigment remaining when the brush is lifted off the painting surface. Another advantage is that when additional markings are applied, as in feathering, the flat finish takes the applied color better.

Usually house paints are sold in quart cans. You may find it awkward to work from these directly, but transferring enough paint for several projects to smaller containers works fine. Basic colors available in flat house paints include black and white (from which you can also make gray) and brown. You may use tube colors and tints to achieve reds, blues, yellows and other colors. This combination of house and tube paints is my personal preference. In any case, remember that it is easier to make the flat finish of a completed piece glossy (if you desire it) than to tone down a glossy finish to a soft luster.

SELECTING YOUR COLORS

If you have never painted a bird carving, start with a species that possesses a relatively simple pattern. Among the birds shown in this book that are suitable for a beginner are the Barn Swallow (Plate 2), Red-breasted Nuthatch (Plate 6), Rufous-sided Towhee (Plate 10) and Scarlet Tanager (Plate 13). I have decided to give step-by-step instructions for the Barn Swallow for two reasons. First, this bird is one of our most widely distributed, best-known songbirds; and, secondly, it is the only bird in this book shown "on the wing" (this bird seems to be constantly in flight, and I could not bring myself to show it otherwise!). Carvings of flying birds require a little less detail work and make easier painting projects. The following instructions will also serve to suggest the general procedure for painting any bird carving. (For those who want to begin with the Fox Sparrow, another familiar songbird, detailed instructions may be found in my book *Carving Popular Birds*, Dover 26136-0.) After the instructions for painting the Barn Swallow, I have provided a list of specific colors you will need for painting the fifteen other birds. Remember that this list is not fixed and absolute; many colors can be created by mixing others. The following colors, however, are fairly basic and are needed for all or at least most of the species illustrated:

1. White.
2. Black.
3. Burnt umber. (With flat house paints you must

check color samples, as each manufacturer may market several brown shades under different trade names. An example is Cook & Dunn's "Cape Cod Brown," an excellent dark brown once a small amount of black has been added.)

4. Burnt sienna.
5. Raw sienna.
6. Red. (Note: Most tube colors that look like "fire-engine red" are sold under such trade names as "Grumbacher red," "Winsor red," etc. Be sure to check color samples before purchasing.)
7. Ultramarine blue. (Check paint samples available; other types of blue, such as Prussian blue or cobalt blue, may be more suitable to your immediate needs.)
8. Cadmium yellow medium. (The various yellows should all be considered, depending on the species being painted. Yellow can be of primary importance in painting warblers and certain other species.)

With the addition of a medium gray (which you may create, of course, by mixing black and white), these colors will provide the painter with the bulk of what he needs. Other colors necessary in smaller quantities include:

9. Indian red or red oxide.
10. Raw umber.
11. Payne's gray.
12. Olive green.
13. Cadmium orange medium. (Whenever possible, I prefer to create the desired shade of orange by mixing cadmium yellow medium with red.)

Besides actual paints, a wide variety of colors is available in tints. The Rich Lux Products Company of Philadelphia puts out an excellent line known as "Minit Tint." The beauty of tints is that, since they contain no hardeners or driers, they have an extremely long shelf life under moderate temperature conditions. Be sure to follow instructions to determine the maximum amount of tint that can be safely used. Applying too much will prevent proper drying.

BEFORE YOU BEGIN

After you have sanded your carving to a smooth finish, it is necessary to seal the wood. Clear wood sealers include lacquer and shellac. Two coats are usually sufficient. Sand between coats with #220 or finer sandpaper. Wood that contains knots needs to be carefully sealed, as the resins in knots will discolor paint.

Once it has been sealed, your carving should be primed. Priming further protects the wood and provides a uniformly pigmented surface to paint on. Remember to use oil-based primer when you are painting with oils, acrylic primer when you are using acrylic paints. When you paint with acrylics, you may want to start with an oil primer and then coat this with acrylic primer. Acrylic primer applied directly to the wood raises the grain, an effect you may prefer. This requires more sanding, but it allows the natural beauty of the grain to show through.

"Kilz," made by Masterchem Industries, is an excellent product that I recommend. Since this is a primer-sealer, it allows you to prime and seal in one operation, saving you a step. Best of all, it can be covered with either oils or acrylics. When using acrylics, however, it is a good idea to top it with a coat of acrylic primer.

While brushing on any coat of primer, be sure not to leave ridges or brush marks, the presence of which will make painting of details more difficult later on. After the primer has dried, sand a final time with #220 or finer sandpaper. This will remove any roughness, providing a smooth base to paint over.

NOTE: Read and follow the instructions found on the labels of all primers, sealers and paints you may use. Familiarize yourself with the qualities of each product as well as precautions necessary for their safe use.

PAINTING A SONGBIRD CARVING— STEP BY STEP

Now you are ready to paint your songbird carving. The following detailed procedures for painting a male Barn Swallow in spring plumage, a brightly colored bird with only a few different areas of color, will give you a good idea of how to go about painting any songbird. It is advisable to read through all the instructions first, before actually mixing or applying any paint.

Referring to Plate 2, outline on your carving the boundaries of the major feather areas and the eyes, using an ordinary lead pencil. Do not indicate any finer details at this time. Always paint the areas that have lighter, brighter colors first, in this case the buff body and underwing coverts (wing linings). If by accident you make the buff too extensive, you can always paint over it in blue-black, whereas if you need to paint over blue-black with buff, it is difficult to retain a strong buff finish.

The buff color of the underside of the body and the wing linings is created by mixing a small amount of white with raw sienna. Usually two coats are necessary, especially if you are using acrylic paints. Remember to refer to the color plate as you paint. Once you have covered this basic color area you may highlight feather details with a lighter buff, made by adding white to a portion of your basic color. If dark edges of individual groups of feathers are desired, you may make the right shade by adding more raw sienna to the basic buff color.

Next, mix black, white and blue to make a blue-gray and paint the underside of the primary and secondary flight feathers. Again, by using more white in the mixture you can highlight feather detail; black added to the basic mixture can produce a darker shade useful for delineating shadows where feathers overlap.

Now paint the rust-red areas over the bill on the lower forehead and on the chin and throat. You have a number of options for obtaining this color. You can simply use Indian red or red oxide unmixed; you can add a little red to burnt sienna; or you may even be able to create the right shade by adding black to red. My own preference is the mixture of burnt sienna and a little red. After this has dried you can add a very small amount of raw sienna to the basic color and use it to highlight the "cheek" area. As you go, keep referring to the plate and any other reference sources you possess to determine the exact shades of color you need.

The underside of the tail can now be painted. The white areas on top and bottom should be painted first, at least roughly (you can touch up the details later), using a couple of thin washes of white. This way, you will not have to apply the white over a much darker color, which would be difficult to cover properly. I have provided a separate top view of the tail as a guide to this stage of painting. Once you have finished applying the white, define the edges of the color areas very lightly with a fine-pointed pencil. After this is done, mix a dark blue-gray and apply it to the undersurface of the tail. Lighter and darker shades of this basic mixture will again allow you to define feather detail—even, as you become more adept at it, enabling you to rival what could be done with wood-burning techniques.

You are now ready to paint the most extensive color area of all, that which extends from the head over the entire upper side of the body and wings, including the lores and narrow throat band. The blue-black mixture desired for this is really a "midnight blue." You may wish to add more blue to this for highlights on the crown, behind the eye and elsewhere. I cannot over-emphasize the importance of supplementing your reference sources with personal observation of live birds. Only this way will you understand the finer hues and shadings. Observing Barn Swallows on the wing is not easy, as they are constantly diving and twisting in rapid flight, but sometimes a high wind will "hold" them as they turn into it. Your personal research in the field should be an integral part of your painting (as of your carving) efforts. It's fun, too!

Now use a very fine-pointed brush to paint the eyes in black, brown and white. Touch up the white areas on the tail. Finally, paint the bill (a delicate area it is always wise to save for last). Simply use black, applying it smoothly to complement the underlying texture of the wood. Congratulations! If you have correctly followed all instructions and the color plate, you should now be looking at a fully painted carving of a flying Barn Swallow.

A word of caution to those who are painting carvings with wood-burned feather detail: make sure that the paint you use is of a consistency thin enough not to clog the fine details of feathering that you have so laboriously striven to create.

With practice you will acquire familiarity with the effects of different paints, tools and procedures. Do not strive for speed; it will come on its own. Depending on the degree of realism you desire, the color schemes shown on the plates can be either simplified or refined through further research and observation. Good luck!

For your convenience, the colors of the paints needed for the carvings illustrated on Plates 1 and 3 through 16 are given below. Remember, however, that pigments vary from manufacturer to manufacturer and with the type of paint. In many cases you will need to experiment with different mixtures to achieve a particular color. Some of the colors listed may be created by mixing others. And you may work out any number of satisfactory substitutions. The following list is intended only as a rough guide.

LIST OF COLORS

Plate 1. Mourning Dove: Black; white; burnt umber; raw sienna; raw umber; blue; red.

Plate 3. Northern Mockingbird: Black; white; burnt umber.

Plate 4. Downy Woodpecker: Black; white; red.

Plate 5. Horned Lark: Black; white; burnt umber; raw sienna; raw umber; burnt sienna; cadmium yellow medium.

Plate 6. Red-breasted Nuthatch: Black; white; burnt umber; burnt sienna; Payne's gray.

Plate 7. Fox Sparrow: Black; white; burnt umber; burnt sienna; cadmium yellow medium.

Plate 8. American Redstart: Black; white; burnt umber; blue; orange.

Plate 9. White-throated Sparrow: Black; white; burnt umber; burnt sienna; cadmium yellow medium.

Plate 10. Rufous-sided Towhee: Black; white; burnt umber; Indian red.

Plate 11. Great Crested Flycatcher: Black; white; burnt umber; burnt sienna; red; cadmium yellow medium; Payne's gray; olive green.

Plate 12. Eastern Meadowlark: Black; white; burnt umber; raw sienna; cadmium yellow medium; Payne's gray.

Plate 13. Scarlet Tanager; Black; red; cadmium yellow medium; orange.

Plate 14. Mountain Bluebird: Black; white; burnt umber; blue; Payne's gray; ultramarine blue.

Plate 15. Black-throated Blue Warbler: Black; white; burnt umber; Payne's gray; orange; Prussian blue.

Plate 16. Dark-eyed Junco ("Slate-colored" race): Black; white; burnt umber; red; Payne's gray.